I AM

PREDESTINED WOMAN

PREDESTINED

BEAUTY FOR ASHES

COLLECTION

TABLE OF CONTENTS

Forward

Losing your child or children to the foster system is a devastating moment in any Mother's life. Both the Mother and the child are at a loss. A tremendous feeling of emptiness overshadows you; and many questions fill your mind as a mother. Questions you might ask yourself include, "Will I ever see my children again?" "Do I have what it takes to meet all of these requirements that await me?" "Will they like their foster parents more than me?"

All the aforementioned questions and many more are the reality of women who walk this path every day, but are able to face the challenges and welcome their children back home.

One such lady is the author of this book, The Predestined Woman. She has walked the walk; and now, in her book titled, "I Am Predestined Beauty for Ashes" she will share her story. As she shares her story, "None Are Loss", this book will capture your heart.

This story is her testimony on how God gave her beauty for ashes. I had the pleasure of witnessing the many challenges she faced, which included surviving the dark world of domestic violence. She did not allow her inner scars to hinder her future opportunity to love again. One by one she was able to overcome it because of her strong relationship with Jesus Christ. She is a passionate voice who can talk the talk with confidence because she walked that walk. She will let each woman know," I made it, and you can too!"

She is an amazing wife, mother and minister of God's Word. Most of all she is a true inspiration for anyone who meets her. When she hears the word, "No" she patiently & prayerfully finds another opportunity or way to get the job done. She does not quit at the first sign of a struggle. Her experiences have made her into a strong advocate.

I was blessed to meet her about 8 years ago as her home visitor. My job was to come into her home to support her and her children. 'I wanted to offer her all that our agency had. I was hoping to empower her life for the better. Now that I look back over the years, I realize she changed my life, she empowered me, and most of all she left a permanent mark on my life; letting me know: "When life gives you lemons, don't just make lemonade; take the time to bake some lemon cookies.

With all sincerity & respect,

Sherri-Lee Tolbert,

Early Headstart Educator

Introduction

A lot of women walking the streets talking to themselves are experiencing more pain, heartache, hurt and abuse than, most have in their lifetime on a day to day basis.

Many of them loss their children to Children Family Services due to unforeseen circumstances and decisions. These women are feeling hopeless and broken inside replaying the moment they wish they had the power to change. Some find themselves living in a homeless shelter or domestic violence home. Others are going through it silently in our own communities showing up to work with the biggest smile, outgoing and full of potential but when they leave, they are fighting for survival or fighting to want to survive because they are mothers without their children.

God fills our mouth weekly with the Word of Life. Often, we give it to people who already see for themselves that He is Christ.

The Word of Christ is The Word of Life to those who believe. There are many women, children and families that need to hear His Word.

As you read this book a mother is preparing to face the Judge to receive the courts determination of her ability to nurture her children according to the requirements of Child Welfare Laws. Men are taking advantage of young women who are looking for a kind word of validation that can erase all the things they think about themselves because of what they are going through.

When we act and began to help the women we encounter, we save generations from the entrapments of hopelessness, feelings of abandonment and the pains of abuse.

I wrote this book for women who need to know God gives Beauty for Ashes.

This Introduction is for whoever needs to know the power of their message, work and ministry. Those who need to hear something that will ignite them to break past the fear, never ending preparation and one system fits all mentality, to start transporting multitudes into their destiny.

I had to break through the cycles that tell us we are doing great things even when we are not doing what we are chosen and anointed to do. Every week I led women who are devoted to the Gospel of Christ in prayer and Bible Study. Women that have the potential to go out and reach others with their own message of redemption and salvation.

Month after month we encouraged one another but stayed in a vicious cycle that encumbered us from fulfilling our purpose because we were not reaching others we were preaching to the choir. I had to come to the realization that God rescued me from the pit of despair intending for me to go back and bring others out of that very same pit because He showed me the way out. In my secret place I prayed for the protection and safety of children in foster homes and throughout my day I encouraged women to keep God first and see themselves the way God sees them.

Now through this book I am returning to the pits that attempted to keep me from my purpose and I AM reaching in to help other women like me. By using my experiences and the message God fills my mouth with to support and uplift women whose children are in Children Family Service's temporary placement due to domestic violence, abuse and neglect. I stand with them and if you stand with them, I stand with you.

Chapter 1

"NONE ARE LOSS"

My children were removed from my home and placed in a foster home a little over eight years ago. Looking at us now you would never know we experienced separation. We are lively and vibrant and our love for one another is sincere with a bond that runs deep. My children look like they grew up in the church all their lives. They do not have the profile of children who were ward of the court like I once did. God spared them from the impression abandonment and losing your superhero can leave on a child's mind.

I am now an Ordained Minister and a former County Human Service Coordinating Council

Executive Commissioner. Who would of saw that coming? The woman who was marked incapable of making the right decisions for her children garnered the skills to not only become equipped with all the tools to be the best mom to her children but she emerged from the ashes and became a leader in policy and the pulpit. How is that for a pit to the palace story?

I thank God for the life I now live because I cannot pretend it was accomplished by might nor by power. I cannot ignore the fact that I had no will to go forward so self-will could not create my outcome. God is the catalyst to my change, and I honor Him by not locking the name Jesus behind my teeth. I realized when social services removed my children that I wanted them to know no matter who lets them down they are loved by the truest love this universe has ever known and that is the LOVE OF JESUS.

I now know the pain my children and I experienced in our lives had purpose. God gives Beauty for Ashes. He Predestined our Beauty but not the ashes. Choices and decisions, we make cause the ashes. Warning signs and rules, we choose to ignore give way to the offenses we encounter. Looking back, I can see things I could have done differently that would have stopped my children from being taken away. However, I thank God he does not waste anything.

God does not look down on us when we fall into a pit, ridiculing us while covering the hole with a large stone of regret. God's love is relentless. He sends someone to find us that will help lift us out and set us on the right path. We may not understand the path that we are on but if we are willing to listen He will guide us in the direction of our Purpose. He sees you for who you really are and the things you will one day do. For me that day is now.

Over the past several years I helped women reunify with their children restore their homes and maintain safe permanency. I also have the pleasure of speaking with foster moms, helping them understand the purpose power and potential they carry to empower the youth they take into their homes to overcome the challenges that come with instability and being separated from their families.

I help people grow an intimate relationship with The Lord Jesus Christ rooted in their desire to know Him as FIRST PLACE. When we put God first everything else takes a backseat. When we truly give God first place in our lives His mercy (getting a lesser consequence than you deserve) and His grace (unmerited favor) rule the outcome.

Have you ever heard someone say, "The Blood of Jesus Cover Me?" This is a request for God's Mercy, Grace and Sovereignty. The Blood of Jesus covers every aspect of who you are. Your past, present and future. Your health, wealth and spirit. Your lineage, legacy and prosperity. The list goes on and on. The statement is literally telling death to pass over you and everything connected to you in exchange for God's Mercy, Grace and Sovereign Will. This is what God did for me and I pray through this book you receive the information you need to accept the invitation of Jesus Christ so you can one day say, "God did it for me so He can do it for You."

Romans 8:31 KJV

What shall we then say to these things? If God be for us, who can be against us?

Right now, it seems one decision has the power to take everything and leave you standing alone. Your life is upside down, no one seems to understand what you are going through. You have become oppressed by the thought of being unequipped to do anything to fix the brokenness. To bring your kids home. To convince the courts that your kids need you and you need your kids. Everything was snatched away from you without warning. I understand. My children went into the care of Child Protective Services while I could do nothing but be examined by Emergency Medical Technicians. The bruising lulled me to sleep to recuperate, rendering me helpless. How can I sleep I need to find my children? There is no time for recuperating. I need to pick up the pieces and put my life back together. I feared returning to my house because I was sure he would catch me there and end my life. With my Dad's help I packed a few things before beginning my journey.

Fear caused me to walk away from everything I owned and never return to the familiar. My life may not have looked like much to begin with to anyone looking in, but it was mine. My life. Thoughts and questions haunted my mind. Where are my children? Are they scared? Are they in a home together? When can we be together again? The most devastating thought "I may never get my children back." Are you burdened with these same questions? I am here to tell you; you can release those humiliating thoughts right now. You can turn this moment into a RESET. If one decision has the power to take everything, then another decision has the power to give it all back with increase.

Can you imagine looking back on the day that caused you so much grief and pain thinking, "That day made me find my strength." What if the experience could cause you to understand your resilience? What if the questions extended you an invitation to define your purpose? Imagine you look back and realize the yearning taught you to seek who you are and whose you are. You realize the emptiness gave you room to become the best version of yourself. I am talking about discovering your greatest potential through choosing to reset your life.

You discover THE REAL YOU and learn to value you, despite all that happened and what anyone has to say about it. The immediate benefit to this self-discovery is you now realize the potential inside of you to take command over your life and the lives of your children. You accomplish reunification with safe permanency. Proving that you are what is in the best interest of your children.

Are you ready? To restore, rebuild and renew you? The decision to undergo change will no longer feel mandated or forced because you are making the choice to pursue every opportunity presented to you, to reclaim your life and make it what it is PREDESTINED to be.

Romans 12:1-2 KJV

I beseech you therefore, brethren, by the mercies of God, that ye present your bodies a living sacrifice, holy, acceptable unto God, which is your reasonable service. And be not conformed to this world: but be ye transformed by the renewing of your mind, that ye may prove what is that good, and acceptable, and perfect, will of God.

When I started to write about losing my kids to Children Family Service, I began to write how it all happened. I wrote about what he said, what I did, why it went that far and everything in between. Then I remembered when I reach out to women and encourage them to take their life back. I share with them that I have been where they are.

I tell them about how beautiful my kids have grown and what it took to get them home, but I do not shine a flood light on the abuse or the abuser. Why because it does not matter.

Talking about that one occasion cannot tell the whole story. The courts do not write down in their reports. "Blunt force kicks to her lady parts got the children removed from the home. No, the courts are concerned with the guardians' mindset. Will the children be neglected? Is this a safe environment for the children? Are you able to make the right decisions for the children's well-being? Bottom line, are you capable of keeping the children safe?

We become so devastated about what happened that we focus on all the wrong things. We began to speak of the abuse, our heartbreak, the hurt and betrayal. We are describing the decay of a broken home. Then we size up the enemy that made himself comfortable in our territory. We describe the stature of the enemy, His mannerisms and nature we become ambassadors proclaiming his record of undefeated titles. Deeming ourselves unable to defeat him. Victim to his tactics.

I am not talking about any one person and we will get into that later. I am speaking of how hopelessness and the spirit of heaviness causes us to murmur and complain about all the things necessary to cease what is already ours. Sometimes we get so caught up in how big or serious the issue is that we began to speak to ourselves and others about what we are going through, how we got there and when it all started.

Getting caught up in explaining the scenery, what we said, what they said, and how it made us feel instead of focusing on the promise.

Are you repeating how it all happened over and over again in your mind? Become transformed by the renewing of your mind. Change your focus. Do not replay what happened instead rehearse what is going to happen. Began to envision yourself strong again. Your children, happy, whole and free. Proclaim the outcome you desire and are passionate about seeing manifest in your life. Meditate on the results being in your favor that you may prove what is that good, and acceptable, and perfect will of GOD.

Transformation begins in the mind. God wants us to declare He is the God of our battles and battlegrounds. He is able to return our children into our arms safely without any further harm and stop the recidivism that usually follows even on to the next generation. If you are ready the pain can end right now. God can put a freeze to any further damage and began to reverse the outcome right now. I mean today.

We do not have to grieve what has been temporarily set aside for us to take ownership over. People grieve what they loss. You have not lost anything. You are at the beginning of something new. Your outlook sets the tone of your outcome. I know you are crying, mad, and frustrated. You are either mad at them or mad at yourself or both. I am saying do not waste your energy. Dry your face and pick yourself back up. Not because I said, because your kids need you.

You may feel like this is a losing battle. The enemy is trying to convince you "they will never give your kids back to you." "They get paid to keep your kids away from you." I am here as living proof to prove to you they will give your kids back to you. Not because the system is great and full of nice understanding people, just waiting to give you a second chance. No, because God is great, and He is Notorious at giving second chances. You may be saying, "I already had a second chance." Great news, God's definition of second chance is not like mans. Second chance simply means redo. Yes, you can do it again.

I must say it again, do not spend time mourning. The enemy comes to steal, kill, and destroy but Jesus comes that we may have life and that more abundantly.

People will give you the energy you give off. If you are miserable, sharing war stories then like the old sane goes misery loves company. People will give you a shoulder to cry on and tell you they have been where you are. They will tell you about their aunt, cousin, friend, coworker that lost their kid and went through hell trying to get them back. They will share how much they hate the system and everyone who put you through this. If you show them pain, they will try to numb it with any vice they have in their toolbox. Everything, ranging from talking to clubbing, drinking, sex, and drugs. I must give it to you straight because this is not the time to be pacified. You need to stay woke. Do not call for their shoulder pull on their faith. I mean PULL!

Cause them to proclaim the victory by showing up with a renewed mind. Show them, the things I use to do I don't do no more. The places I use to go I don't go no more. The way I use to talk I don't talk no more. Do a complete turnaround. Why? Because your kids need you and you need your kids. God believes in you and He is asking you to believe in Him so you can once again believe in yourself. Speak the victories you are going toc achieve and live everyday expecting reunification. This is your redo.

The process is for you. Do you know that God could have taken the children of Israel directly into the promise land? He intentionally took them in a different direction because He had to work the faith in their heart. He knew they would fear the fight ahead and go back to the bondage they were used to.

God PREDESTINED for them to live in a land of milk and honey. Milk represents your needs being met and Honey represents the desires. The place God Predestined for them to live was going to meet their needs and desires. I had to realize even when I was with my kids we were not living in a land of milk and honey. Our needs and desires went unmet physically, mentally, spiritually and emotionally. God wanted more for us then waking up day by day not knowing what to expect. Trying but never accomplishing and building, living, growing but without purpose.

I worked and went to school, but I did not have any clear goals set for either. My kids had me, but my love was strained by past hurts, current abuse and a lot of bad guidance. My children lived in a constant state of instability with uncertainty but when I hit RESET everything changed from the inside out. I did not have to have a lot for my children to see my love for them is authentic and my smile is genuine. On the first visit my children could see and feel the difference. I was not scared; my eyes were bright, and I was attentive to each one of them. I knew I was embarking on something new. I radiated things are going to be different this time without having to say a word. This was my redo.

Put it all behind you, whatever they did, you did, you are no longer that person. Sure, the courts are judging you. The social worker glares at you and sees you as nothing more than what she read on a report.

True or not stop defending yourself it makes you look defensive and full of self-denial. Own what happened by not becoming what you are going through but instead allowing it to transform you to who you want to be. Then prove you will no longer stand for mediocrity in any area of your life through actions not your words. Could you have done more to protect your children? Absolutely! We all have room to grow. When your child is snatched away from everything they know and put in a home with strangers. No parent has room to say I did all I could. A parent takes the blame and drops everything and everyone. Our children become our primary focus. That is what a parent does. We own it. What they did, what we did and the consequences that come from it. Then we choose to do better when given the chance. This is your chance.

Chapter 2

My Dad took me back to my house to pack before I left my home for good. I didn't know where I was going to go or how I was going to make it on my own. I just knew my home was no longer a safe place.

When I walked in my house the emptiness caused a pain so severe my eyes swelled with tears. I could hear my heart saying, "They are gone, my children are gone, and I am helpless to do anything to get them back."

The thought of my children being in a foster home caused childhood pain to resurface and I realized nothing changed. I repeated the same cycle! my kids are scared and alone wondering where am I and when am I going to come get them? Counting the minutes, hours and days waiting for someone to tell them I am on my way. This is no one's fault but mine. I did this!

This agony was worse than all the emotional, physical and sexual abuse I experienced in my relationships and throughout my life. This internal physical and emotional grieving felt like my womb turned into a bag of poisonous blood. My motherhood was eroding away from the inside out. I called out to Jesus because the pain forced me to admit I know HIM. No more was I questioning if I believed and what does it mean to believe. Wasting time because I had time to waste.

This pain pushed the name JESUS out of my mouth because by no other name I know can a man be saved, and I needed saving. I could roll up in a fetal position and just die in agony. Die from self-inflicted wounds caused by mistake after mistake.

I did not want my life to end that way. My kids needed me or maybe I just needed my kids. What do I have to offer them? I failed to protect them. Maybe God chose someone to give them what I never could?

 At that moment I saw myself wandering the streets homeless and insane. Out of my mind, twiddling my fingers, mumbling about the kids I used to have. That was the only future left for me. The thought scared me, but I still clung to my resurrected desire declaring even there I would still want to talk to Jesus about my kids. Even still, I would need his spirit to rock me in the back of the gas station while I curled up under a box.

I still need him. I recommitted my children, feeling unworthy I recommitted my raggedy self and repented for every wrong I ever did.

Do you know you need Jesus?

As I sat there with my face in my hands leaning into my lap I said to God, "My children are alone." I never taught them about you. I am talking to you because I know you, but they don't know you." I felt I let my children down in the worse way imaginable by not teaching them about Jesus.

Now is the time to recommit to Him.

RECOMMIT

Say it with me, Jesus I need you, I need you to stay next to me. Please be with me in everything I say, everything I do and everything, I think. I cannot do this without you and most importantly I do not want to. Help me through this. I know you will see me through. Jesus Christ, I receive you as my Lord and Saviour please forgive me for everything I did leading up to this moment. I need to know I feel you in my heart. I do believe in you. I believe you can make all things new. Make me new please, I want to be new in you. In Jesus name, Amen.

Now forgive yourself

I forgive myself for everything I ever said, thought and did to others to my children and to myself. I forgive others for what they say, do and think toward me. I forgive them for hurting me, for using me, and for accusing me. I forgive them now. I invite true friendships, fellowships, and counselors into my life. God, I trust you to lead the right people to me and I let go of the people you did not put in my life I release them now. I want to be all you called me to be today, as if I never made a wrong decision or wrong turn. Cloak me in your righteousness and cause me to walk in truth as you lead me in the direction you intend for me. In Jesus name, Amen.

Now pray a prayer of protection over your children.

Bless my children; keep them safe. Protect them from any hurt, harm, or danger. Cover their mind, touch their heart. Watch over them. Provide what they need while they are away. Let them know that this is only for a short time. Wipe their tears from their eyes when they cry. Jesus teach my children how much you love them. Speak your word into their ear even as they sleep. Comfort my children with your spirit and your protection allow no manner of wrong to come near them. Keep them safe. I give my children to you; I commit their lives into your loving hands Father. Show them how much I love them and teach me how to love them even more. Fill me up with your unconditional love for them so they can feel that your love and my love is one. Teach me how to satisfy their every need and what I do not know cause me to learn even as I grow with them and grow in you. Bless them, cover them, protect them and be a Father to them forevermore.

In Jesus name, Amen.

*****

Feel free to continue to talk to God. You do not need a written prayer to speak to Him. You can say whatever you need to say. He is your Father and He loves you and He loves your children. You do not need to know How to pray just talk. If you are asking Him questions and you feel you did not get an immediate answer. Just say "God sew your words in my heart and cause me to walk in obedience." Trust that He answered you and the spiritual ears of your heart will hear the answers as He reveals them to you.

This was a big step forward. You re-committed yourself to believing in yourself again, letting go of all the hurt from the past, not being moved by what people say about you, and you became New in Christ Jesus. Furthermore, you re-committed yourself to being the best mother you can possibly be. To growing with your children and giving them not just your love but the love of their Heavenly Father.

You Are forgiven and you have just successfully committed your family to The God of Heaven and Earth, Jesus Christ His Son and The Comfort of His Spirit.

Congratulations you are my sister and you are not alone.

PURPOSE

PREDESTINED Woman of Purple you are Powerful on Purpose.

Predestined Woman God chose you for His Glory. Your purpose is greater than Nazareth.

You are so much greater than where you are. Although, You may not be where God promised it does not mean you are not right where God wants you.

Your current position does not define your destination. Keep going, keep growing, God's Purpose will prevail.

P.R.E.D.E.S.T.I.N.E.D.

Glory Decree From The Throne Of Grace

I know the Gifts I placed in you.

I see your potential.

Do not discount yourself based off experiences
or opinions.

People pronounce defeat where I authored
Victory. The moves I make and people I use
have a PREDESTINED PURPOSE with ripples
of Eternal Impact.

PURPOSE is flowing behind the scenes but
when Revealed My PURPOSE Recovers ALL.

Chapter 3

After I prayed, I stepped out the room. My Dad said are you okay? I said, "Yes, I am." He said, "while you were in the room I called a friend and told her a little about you she said you can stay with her." I said, "thank you." I looked around my town home for the last time then grabbed the few boxes and things that I packed. I put the stuff by the door. My Dad walked over picked up the boxes and helped me carry my things outside. The lady was in the parking lot with her trunk open. She said, "Hi, are you okay?" I said, "yes I am; thank you." She responded back, "no problem, you can put your boxes in my trunk." As my Dad packed the trunk, he said, "thank you Mimi for coming." He closed the trunk, looked at me and said, "I love you, call me if you need me." As if to say, I will take another 48-hour trip on public transportation if you need me to. I looked at him and said, "thank you Dad."

I felt grateful to have a place to go but I still have a long journey ahead of me. I have to prepare to appear in court.

ENGAGE

Appearing in Court

It takes the strength of God to show up to court. However, showing up to court is critical to your case. The courts do not take absences lightly. The judge will go forward making decisions on your behalf concerning your children and those decisions could take things from bad to worse if you are not present. I remember sitting in court hearing the judge dismiss the legal rights of a parent for not showing up. They no longer had any say in the matter from that moment on. When we recognize God has been gracious, we will show up with grace and humility. Your goal is proving to the court you are what is in the best interest of your children. Nothing else is more important than showing up prepared on purpose and focused. You may have other things in life that are competing for your time and attention but nothing is more important than your kids. Do not allow anything to cause you to miss this appointment.

Reschedule other engagements for another day, if you must, show proof that rescheduling was necessary after court but whatever you do, do not miss court.

Show UP Do Not Show OUT

Going to court without a plan can get really overwhelming very quickly. This is the main place you are going to hear all the information concerning your case, the good, the bad, the ugly and everything in between. Everyone involved in your court case will be there (unless they decided not to show up) The foster parents to your children, all social workers involved. All Biological parents to the children in custody, and the Public Defenders. Including anyone who was invited by any of the parties involved. KEEP CALM and know this is about YOUR CHILDREN. Trust the courts to see through any falsified information. The first court hearing introduces the parties, problems and plot but you get to participate in the PRODUCTION. The end result is up to you and that is the PURPOSE of the hearing. If the decision is fixed and there is nothing you could do about it they would not assign you a to do list. YOU produce your outcome based on the work you put in so no matter what happens today be positive and know there is something you can do, and you can get started right away.

RESPECT THE COURT.

Respect the building. I am talking about the parking lot, to the metal detectors and guards, all the way through the halls, lobby and courtroom. There is not a single place on the court grounds to yell, scream, holler, and cuss someone out. You would be shocked how many people show up to court distraught, yelling and shouting at everyone who works in the building.

 Be presentable, respectable and peaceful. Contrary to popular belief the court workers, public defenders and Judge are not against you. The judge is a mediator the public defender represents you and the guard and receptionist just work at the court. The Judge receives information about all three sides which includes, the county, the children, and the parents. Based off the information a decision is made.

No one knows you, especially not the recommitted you. You may know no one knows you, but do not go around shouting, "You don't know me!" Show them with your calm demeanor and renewed look on life. I am not saying do not care, no you care, but by being calm you show you are eager to do what is right.

Chapter 4

I showed up to court on time not knowing what to expect. I sat in the lobby waiting for someone to call my name. While I was sitting on the bench in the lobby, I noticed a man dressed in a suit speaking to a young woman who was holding her head down. I felt I needed to go over there and speak to them. As I walked over, they lift their heads and I said. "Excuse me, for interrupting but I had to come over here because you sound like The Church." (At the time I had no clue what I meant by that) The man said, we are here because this young lady has court today. She looked at me and said my children are in the system. In a quick turn of events, I began to encourage her. I told her my children are in the system too. They were removed from my home five days ago. But I believe God has a plan for your children and mine. Did you tell your children about Jesus? She shook her head, no. I didn't either. I never told them His name. I believe God wants to give us our children back because now we know what is important. I came over here because I could feel you both know Jesus. If you put God first everything else falls in place. When I got ready to walk away, she said, "excuse me, do you want to go to church tonight? I said, Yes. She said my name is Christa, I said nice to meet you Christa. Then we exchanged phone numbers.

When the judge called my name and I stepped into the courtroom it was highly intimidating. I sat in this long row of people at a table in front of the judge. Everyone began to speak one by one about all the issues concerning the children and my failure at being a good mother. I sat quietly with a peace that surpasses all understanding. They said both of the parents have anger issues and are abusive. Each of them will have to have counseling and services before the children are returned back home. I remember agreeing with their conclusion. We both need counseling. I am not a victim. I became so much of what I've seen, been through and experienced. My Public Defender asked me if I understood and agreed, I said, "yes". When I left, I walked out thinking I have a lot to do and the papers the courts handed me listed my current fix it/to do list.

My to do list.

13 weeks Domestic Violence Counseling

13 weeks Parenting class

Explosive Anger Management

One on One Counseling

Weekly 2 hour supervised visits

I volunteered to attend a women's group throughout this time as well.

RESILIENT

PREDESTINED Woman of Red your Resilience transforms your outcome and the future of all those connected to you.

Predestined Woman God chose you for His Glory. When the enemy comes in like a flood God will Raise a Standard against Him.

Homing in on your destination you are driven.

You are not beat; you are made perfect in weakness.

God wants you to remember He has called you by a new name.

It Glorifies God to Glorify you.

Receive everything that comes with the territory God has given to you.

P.R.E.D.E.S.T.I.N.E.D.

Glory Decree From The Throne Of Grace

Everything meant for your destruction is turned around for your ESTABLISHMENT.

What is supposed to defeat you is Sanctified as a WEAPON of SALVATION that the gates of hell will not prevail against.

The words of your mouth are Purified to Declare My Wonderful Works and bring Salvation to My People.

Your eyes are opened to see Strategies and bring My People the Victory.

You are a comfort to those who seek comfort.

A Refuge To Nations

&

A Sign of Restoration

Chapter 5

When I got back to Mimi's house I realized, I never asked where was the church? What kind of church is it? When does it start? I did not consider how would I get there? I just said, Yes.

I called Christa. she answered the phone, "hello, Hi, I am the girl you met in the court lobby, She said, "Hey, do you still want to go to church tonight?" "Yes, absolutely." Okay, what kind of transportation do you have? "I use the RT." Christa said, "okay, me too, let's meet up at the bus stop." "Okay perfect!" I met up with her and we caught the bus together.

We took the light rail to the transit station and caught 2 more buses to get to the church. When we got to the church, I was half a county away from where I lived. We arrived early and the praise team was rehearsing a song called "He Saw The Best In Me." I never heard the song before so I sat and watched; allowing the words of the song to soak into my mind. When the practice was over, and it was time for Bible Study to begin I recognized the guy who was teaching the Bible study. He was the man with the suit from the court lobby room. He introduced himself to the church as Pastor Allen and then asked everyone to open their Bibles. I did not have a Bible. I did not go to church. I attended church a few times with my aunty a few years ago. But last time I remember attending a church like this I was 14 years old living with my mother.

The music, the message, everything about this church took me back home to where I was safe. Where I was loved. To a time when foster care was something I only knew as a goodwill service to others. Not a generational obstacle I had to learn how to hurdle over.

This church reminded me of the hedge of protection that use to cloak my family. I thought this would be a great place for my children, but my children are in care and I live with a woman I just barely met on the other side of the county. I left that night grateful for the experience but not knowing if I would return.

The next morning Mimi invited me to go with her to celebrate Thanksgiving at her mother's house. When we got to her mom's house, we unpacked the car, dropped off the food and utensils in the kitchen, washed our hands and prepared the food.

I am just one of the ladies helping in the kitchen everything is good, but I began to feel anxious. I step away from the food, wash my hands and slowly walk through the hallway. My eyes catch a teddy bear in one of the rooms and tears start to roll down my face.

I walk back to the kitchen and ask if I could be excused, they say go ahead. I step out the house and take a deep breath. Everything hits me at once. Nothing about these past few days is normal. I am so far away from home. I start walking down the street looking at the houses thinking, my kids could be in any of these houses having Thanksgiving with strangers. I wrap my hands around my lower abdomen, five days ago I woke up with my 3-month-old in my arms. Now, I don't know where she is. Emotions began to flood my mind as I thought about all the suffering I put my children through over the years.

The instability, pain and confusion. Now here we are again. This was not my first time losing my children they went in a receiving home for thirty days as I and the man I was in a relationship with went through voluntary family mediation. I thought it would work, we would both face our demons and become a loving family, but it didn't.

Everyone was still broken, and my children were still living with uncertainty.

Now they are in foster care, in a stranger's home as I try to prove to the court to give me another chance. Why should they? I brought another baby into this chaos. I obviously still haven't learned anything.

As I walked, I cried and groaned in pain. I wanted it all to end. I saw the patterns of my life now become the blueprint of my children's lives. My seven siblings and I went into foster care and my mother and father had to go to court to prove they were able to take care of us. My parents walked away from their home just as I did my town home. My father did not hit my mother and verbally abuse her but my parents had other issues that caused the situation. Going to foster care broke me.

I lost my identity, security and value of self. I wanted a family so bad. I thought I could give them everything I felt I loss. I wanted the ideal family, love, stability and a good home. However, I was broken. I searched for my identity, purpose and stability in love relationships with men. I needed validation.

I needed someone to make me believe in me again. That is what I lost and I was searching desperately for it. The moment I went into foster care I lost my voice. I was treated horribly in multiple different homes and no one believed me. I told people but the moment I realized they did not believe me I never mentioned the incident again. I did not want that for my children.

All types of thoughts flooded my mind. Raindrops fell on my face as tears rolled down my chin. I looked up to the sky and said thank you, for validating my tears.

It is Thanksgiving and people are laughing cooking eating and visiting with their family and you allowed it to rain right here where I am. Thank you, and then I began to sing.

There is Joy

Joy

In the name of The Lord.

There is Joy Joy

In the name of the Lord

The name of the Lord is like a mighty strong tower the name of the Lord is worthy to be praised

The Joy that I have the world didn't give it and the world can't take it away.

I went in circles around the neighborhood singing out loud I did not care who could hear. I told God I will look crazy and talk to myself as long as I was talking to Him and I meant it.

I started singing there's Hope, Faith, Peace.

As I sang The Spirit of The Lord came upon me and I said.

All My kids

My kids

Are in the name of the Lord

All my kids

My kids are in the name of the lord

The name of the lord is like a mighty strong tower the name of the lord is worthy to be praised the kids that I have the world didn't give them and the world can't take them away.

I cried tears of joy as the faith that we were going to be together again arose in me and gave me hope for a better tomorrow.

I said "God you are saying this to me?"

You are giving them back to me!

The Name of The Lord is Jesus and my kids will know you.

When I walked back in the house after I do not know how many laps my faith was restored I believed God just told me press forward because he is returning my kids back to me. I receive it!

ESSENCE

PREDESTINED Woman of White, Essence is The Extraordinary God in You.

PREDESTINED Woman God chose you for His Glory you are made new in Christ.

Keep going until God blesses you with everything, He has promised you.

Do not allow circumstances and other peoples actions or feelings to mar you.

Stay who you are then God can get the Glory and others can learn your story.

Someone needs to know if God did it for you, He will do it for them.

P.R.E.D.E.S.T.I.N.E.D.

Glory Decree from The Throne of Grace

You received me and I received you. Come and feast with me as Royalty.

I have positioned you to receive the best of everything. Although, you did not know me I have known you. When you were okay with little, I caused you to receive abundance. You are elected for I have elected you. You are Glorified come and put on your jewels.

Prepare yourself in your righteous robes do not say you are unworthy for I have chosen you. I alone have perfected you. Are you not perfect? I alone have glorified you. Are you not Glorious? I alone have made you Holy by fulfilling the law. Did I Achieve the VICTORY lawfully? I AM Qualified to proclaim your

Identity. Do you disqualify me?

I AM THAT I AM

And He that sat upon The Throne said, Behold,

I make ALL things new. And He said unto me,

Write: for these words are true and faithful.

Revelations 21:5 KJV

Chapter 6

I continued to attend the church which meant catching the light rail to the transit station and the buses to the church two times a week. I called the counseling services and signed up for my classes. One by one each class returned my call with my start date. I wrote the days in my calendar and attended my classes as scheduled.

In counseling I learned to value myself authentically. Put myself before anyone else; this was a hard concept because as the second eldest of eight children and the oldest daughter, I felt it was my job to look out for my siblings and take care of them.. I made my plate last and cleaned up after ever one was done eating. I went to school, came home and taught my sister everything I learned. I wanted to keep her a step ahead. I did not like the feeling of not understanding a lesson in class so I introduced the topic to her at home, so she was prepared.

 In foster care I was not cared for so on top of caring for others I was taught I was not worth valuing. When I grew to be an adult, I gave the men who complimented me and seem to want me around, everything I owned; because I wanted them to value me. However, I failed to put my children first. I asked the instructors about this concept of me first. I assumed everyone who agreed with it was selfish and were probably raised as an only child. I did not understand. I even mentioned, "how putting yourself first could make anything better. I asked, "how do you put yourself before your children, they are supposed to come first right?" I thought you were going to teach me how to put my children first because I failed at that." The counselor was so patient she said, "no you did not fail to put your children first or anyone else for that matter. That is why you are here; you left nothing for yourself and gave out of an empty barrel." At that time, I did not understand, I just shut up because it sounds right. I knew deep down inside I gave my children everything I had but I did not understand I gave them nothing because I had nothing to give. I only understood something was terribly wrong and my children suffered from it.

Now I realize when we put ourselves first, we have more to give, more to offer, we are not running on empty. We love with the love we have for ourselves and true love and concern for others. Our love becomes strong and authentic and our children benefit from our love for them and ourselves.

When we do not give to ourselves, we use our giving to others to satisfy our insatiable need to be loved. I know because I was like that. It made me an emotional wreck because from the outside I was worth loving I did everything I knew how but, on the inside, I did not love me. I needed someone to say you are worth loving so I could embrace me. I believed that I was just a statistic and because I accepted it my life became the evidence of that. Anyone who seemed to love me I honored and obeyed but when they disapproved of my hair, clothes or the way I looked. I immediately felt ashamed and did whatever I had to do to earn their approval. However, I never received the love I longed for from men in my life. Through engaging in counseling, I realized my desire to be loved was the anchor that kept me in one abusive relationship after another. My need to change for others came from a desire to have the approval of my guardians while in foster care as a teen. I just wanted to be loved and have a family. I went as far as re-evaluating my spiritual beliefs, giving up pork and anything else that the person looked down on even if the thing they looked down on was me. I know you are probably thinking how could you give up on yourself? Every house I moved into in foster care had a new set of rules and a different way of doing things. To stay out of trouble, I had to adapt. I found out through counseling I was still adapting to be accepted. I no longer cared about what I wanted I needed to be what someone else wanted. As I grew up this became my survival technique but what I did not realize is I was not surviving I was destroying myself and taking my children down with me.

The time I spent in counseling taught me how to identify negative learned behaviors, bad relationships and why it is so important to give to yourself first. I still use a lot of the principles I learned through counseling today. The lessons learned in counseling are not given to us to meet the court requirements. They are life skills to map out the blueprint of our lives. To guide us like a compass to where we want to be and who we want to become. To teach our children how to thrive. When I realized I had negative learned behaviors stemming from childhood. I became determined to change. I needed to change but this time into the real me. I spent time with myself getting to know myself. I would ask myself questions like what is your favorite color and favorite food? I listened to my thoughts throughout the day and determined where they came from. Asking myself if they were positive or negative thoughts determining their validity. I wore clothes that made me feel good even if they were not fashionable to anyone else. I stopped adapting by focusing on one thing I need my kids and my kids need ME.

DETERMINE

Predestined Woman of Black you know God is able and He is willing.

Predestined Woman God chose you for His glory. Your Determination makes you a trailblazer.

You have fuel to finish. you accomplish your goal, no matter what the obstacle.

No limitation of your body or circumstance of your situation can stand in your way.

P.R.E.D.E.S.T.I.N.E.D.

Glory Decree from The Throne of Grace

You Hunger and Thirst for righteousness and you are refilled on a daily basis. Your Prayers Release Excellence Satisfying the Soul. Continue to (PRESS) in and I will not cease to fill your cup. You are receiving a double portion anointing with streams of Wisdom that is more than you can contain. The Wisdom overflow is being retained for an ordained time of release. You are overflowing with revelation at all hours of the day. The understanding you receive and visions you see is my presence cloaking your mind and heart from outside interference and influence. I am pouring my word into you. You are sanctified and set apart for my purpose as my vessel unto honor.

STRATEGY

KEEP A SCHEDULE

By now you probably have a lot of classes to attend, appointments to keep and visits with your children that you do not want to miss. You also had a life Before CPS and financial obligations necessary to survive.

All of this may seem overwhelming at first glance and it is, but it is not impossible. Do you remember when you were in high school and you took eight classes a week? This is not very different. We GOT THIS!

You are going to need a DAILY PLANNER. Your daily planner is going to keep track of your weekly agenda. Once you get your daily planner you are going to need to write down all the things you have to attend. Start with your next court date. Then write the classes that you have to take even if you do not know what days. Start listing them anyway so you do not forget to follow up with the necessary departments to start classes.

Write down the visits with your kids and social worker. Keep all important information, appointments and upcoming events in one planner. Do not forget to include work, church and anything else that is important to you and/or guarantees your success.

Write in your daily planner daily. Have a section for note-taking, celebrating accomplishments, write, "Good Job you completed parenting!!" Get ready, one more week until move in day!! Make your planner colorful add stickers. Do whatever you have to do to stay motivated.

Keep records of phone calls

Chapter 7

Every class I attended made me better. Every church service I attended filled me up with love and reassurance of God's promise and kept me going. When I went to church the Leading Lady would always start the service with this song, "How Great is our God."

I heard God telling me every time I walked in the service and she song that song. I will sing this song with my children standing beside me. How great is Our God, Yes, our God. My children will know God as Our God they will know Jesus as their Saviour and The Holy Spirit as their Wonderful Counselor. I sang the song like it was a private conversation between me and heaven. The words became life and had purpose and intention. I song with passion. Expecting the words of my praise to turn into a pen and extend my visitation from supervised to overnight stays. I waved my hands side to side shifting the tables in my favor. I expected praise to do just what God said it would do. Bind the strong man with fetters of iron remove my enemies out of my way so I can walk into my blessings.

Praise and Worship is where I forged my battlegrounds. I stomped my feet like a drum as God fought my enemies and enlarged my territory. As I sang, *How Great Is Our God*, I believed God would send His Angels to encamp around the home my children and I would one day call home. I said, *God You Are*

Bigger Than My Problems And Circumstances.
I did not care that the praise team already moved on to the next set of lyrics. I never concerned myself with what others thought because I am a mother and I am going home empty. This is the place I send the praises of my mouth out to do what I cannot. *How Great is Our God, All Will See..* I was hooked on the hook; *God You Are Holy, I Know You As Sovereign.* I submitted my case to The God of Heaven And Earth through my praises as I declared, "nothing is too hard for You." I only have this moment when I leave, I am facing battles I am not equipped to fight alone. This praise is my down payment on the favor I will borrow later. Praise is my weapon because my mind is not clever enough to bring my kids

home and actions by themselves are not enough.

BUT GOD, HE can make a way where there is no way. ALL WILL SEE HOW GREAT IS OUR GOD My feet got to moving and I danced right where I stood. I believed one day all will see, How Great is Our God when my children are standing praising next to me. I will be a living breathing testimony of His abounding mercy like the stories we read about in the Bible. People looked at me in amazement. They never could understand what a young girl like me could go on and on about. Like I said, I did not have time to appease their curiosity. One day the miracle of my children standing next to me will speak for me. I am dancing alone but soon I will dance to the synchronized motions of my children.

I love attending the services because I knew without a shadow of a doubt, I did not bring myself to this church way across the county on my own I was being ushered by God. I did not find these people on my own. Every step was God's hand revealing His master plan for the lives of my children. He was giving me another chance I did not deserve.

I have a reason to Praise!

One day when church was ending, I received a call as I stood in the lobby, It was Mimi the lady who took me in. She said Hi, how was church?

I said, good. She said that is good, I am calling because my sister needs me now and I need to make room for her. She really needs my help and I am expecting her to come in the morning. I said okay," I understand thank you for everything I know how important it is to be there for your sister I would do the same. Thank you for your support through this." She said, are you going to be okay, I wish there was something I could do. I said I am going to be fine. Thank you, you have done a lot for me. Thank you. When I hung up.

Almost instinctively, I called one of the ladies whom I attend women's group with and told her my situation. She said you can come stay with us we have women's group in the morning, can you get here now? I said yes, I will just catch the light rail there instead of North. She said, okay, see you soon. When I hung up the phone, I said, thank you Jesus, in an excited whisper. The Leading Lady said, is everything okay? I said, yes, everything is great! I was told I must leave the person whose house I stayed at, because her little sister is coming and she needs her big sister now. Her little sister is facing some challenges.. The leading lady said, oh no, are you okay? Yes, I just called one of the sisters from the women group I attend, and she said I can come and stay. She said, oh Good! Yes, I am going there tonight. She said, Praise God.

In the morning I got up and got ready for our women group; it was so awesome to be with people who are the same in every way in this season of our lives. We talked about Jesus all the way to the women's group; we talked about what we learned all the way back and shared stories about our children all throughout the day including some of the challenges we face on this uphill battle.

I had a temporary place to rest and a long schedule of classes to attend I went to Anger Management on Monday afternoon, Tuesday, Parenting and in the evening supervised visits with my children for two hour, Wednesday Midweek Service at church, Thursday, Women Group and Thursday evening, Domestic Violence.

I still had time to attend every service at my new church home including Tuesday & Thursday prayer and special conferences.

If we begin to doubt ourselves and feel like we must go back then that means that we are closer to the summit than the valley. Claudia Vidal

In between church services I faced a lot of challenges and went through a lot of mental and emotional ups and downs. No one really knows what someone experiences from Sunday to Sunday. I was fighting depression and thoughts of giving up. I knew I could not stay at Angela's house indefinitely. Every day I hopped on the bus on my way to my classes I pondered. How am I going to get my kids back? Every single day brought with it a different set of challenges of its own. It felt like I spent my mornings climbing various types of mountains and my nights crossing dry grounds with venomous creatures to get to my children. Nothing was ever simple. My thoughts were even chaotic, "*I want my kids, but I do not have a house, I need to get a house but I do not have a job, I should get a job but I have a to do list that causes me to be booked majority of the week. I cannot afford to miss a court appointment by being stuck to a work schedule and I need to stay available to see my kids*".

I felt all alone when I focused on my issues and focusing on them too much caused anxiety. I had nausea, chills and an upset stomach while staying at Angela's house. Just the thought of being sick while she was trying to help me by allowing me to stay at her house made me annoyed which caused the symptoms to progress. I felt like an ungrateful house guest.

While I laid there sick, I got a call from the Leading Lady she asked me where I was. I told her I was at Angela's house from the women's group but for some reason I was not feeling good. She said, the Pastor and I are coming to get you. I said, Really? She responded, Me and the Pastor were praying about it and we both agree you should stay with us. I was shocked, grateful and without words. She said, do you want to stay with us? Yes!

They picked me up that night and I stayed with the Pastor and Leading Lady for three months. Throughout the three months I left early in the morning with the leading lady and her son. I caught the light rail to my counseling classes and got picked up in the evenings to go to the church services.

I began to look for apartments in the area that I could raise my children in. I filled out applications for many apartments, but my income did not qualify.

I continued to name and claim apartments until God told me to be specific and ask for what I want.

So, I did.

One day while riding the bus I wrote out exactly what I wanted.

If you knew you had a date and time that you would achieve your goal, you would be more willing to stick it out through the rough times. Stay focused. Stay committed. That day IS coming! Behave as you expect it to happen, and it will. Kathy Kidd

ENCOURAGE

Predestined Woman of Yellow The Joy of The Lord is your strength and The Hope of Glory is where you place your confidence.

 PREDESTINED Woman God chose you for His Glory You don't give in to doubt.

A little place to position your foot is all you need to stand on Faith.

You draw your strength, your joy and your power from a well deep within that never runs dry.

P.R.E.D.E.S.T.I.N.E.D.

Glory Decree From The Throne Of Grace

I grace your words with sweetness as rich as honey to remove the breaches that limit my people from receiving the life, I prepared for them. Your words carry my purpose do not hold back.

The pureness of your message is refreshing to the hearer that will hear and those who listen will receive more than their share. Do not change your words to conform to their ears. Their ears may be converted and transformed by your words. My revelation has become your reality and your words are worship in Spirit and in Truth.

you are my gardener planting the seed I will increase. Keep imprinting, My Word is your witness confirming you do not declare of yourself.

Isaiah 52:7 KJV

How beautiful upon the mountains are the feet of him that bringeth good tidings, that publisheth peace; that bringeth good tidings of good, that publisheth salvation; that saith unto Zion, Thy God reigneth!

EQUIPPED

KEEP RECORDS

Always keep a journal and pen on you; you never know when you may need to write something down or feel the need to journal.

Keep records of your attendance for every class, counseling, meeting and thing that you do.

Be respectful to your caseworker; even if they are not respectful to you, still be respectable.

Update contact information. I was constantly moving around, but I made sure I told my worker where I was, and mentioned at least one accomplishment, then stated a thing I was working toward. When applicable I asked a reasonable question.

Example voicemail: Hi May, this is (your full name) I am currently staying at (complete address) my phone number is (area code 456-0987) I have two classes left of Parenting and I plan to continue the classes with the instructors' permission. I have really enjoyed the visits with my children in the office. Do I have any other requirements before I receive unsupervised visits with my children? Thank you for your time. You can call me back at (123-456-0987)

You can never be too nice when speaking to a caseworker who is overloaded with cases and screaming parents.

Chapter 8

The social worker over my case scheduled a visit to come talk to me. She asked, what have I been doing? I laid out the list I even handed her my certificates she was willing to help because in five months I completed all that was required of me, but I choose to continue the counseling classes.

I was still attending the court ordered explosive anger management and the non-mandated women group. I never missed a visit with my children. She talked to me about unsupervised visits and a nice program that will help me locate a place.

When I met the program manager I showed him the certificates I received from completing my classes. He said, "why are those still in the folder in your bag? The moment you get in the apartment we are going to buy you frames to put those on the wall."

First thing I said is wait, I can put things on my walls? He answered back, of course! Especially, your certificates and He began to count them. He said, we are going to need a lot of picture frames. I smiled because in this small room, this was the first time I was recognized for an achievement since being separated from my parents as a child.

When I received my certificates, it was more like a line up. The facilitators handed them out like a handshake. They never stopped moving the line to recognize the individual accomplishments of each parent fighting for their children.

When I showed my certificates to my social worker and my public defender they were submitted as evidence not an accomplishment. Just another thing to check off the list and move the case forward. However, the program manager saw my hard work, perseverance and determination. Even if he didn't he said just enough for me to pause and see it for myself. I took a deep breath and that is when it hit me, I just got a home for my children!

Within less than a month after the conversation with the social worker. I secured our home through the program. I finished my classes, applied for a job and started working immediately. I got approved for overnight stays; I chose Saturday evenings, and my children attended church with me Sunday morning in the front row singing, "How Great is Our God."

SERENE

PREDESTINED Woman of Royal Blue you know how to arrest the emotions that flood within and do what you must do when no one else can.

PREDESTINED Woman God chose you for His Glory Your Peace is who you are not what you have.

You do not have to lift your voice except to sing.

You can make a Decree and the storm will have to cease.

Serene The Daughter of The King

P.R.E.D.E.S.T.I.N.E.D.

Glory Decree From The Throne Of Grace

The world desires you but I keep you near. You are the evidence of my presence. Everything that is wrong is set right when you activate My Sovereignty.

Remain in tune with My Word, My Singular Will. You know my voice; you recognize my sound. You are keen to my essence. You realize my works. Keep watching me and I will show you great and marvelous things, I will unveil the strategies and plots that seek to hinder you and those around you. I will uncover the smokescreens, unmask the puppets and reveal to you my Glory.

You will enter places that I reserved for My Spirit. I will make you ruler over territories to position My People and decree My Will. You will birth out nations in lands of fruitfulness. You will be exalted, and I will be exalted in you. Remain who you are, and I will tell you great and marvelous things you did not know I will reveal the unseen to you.

BUILD AND PRESENT YOUR CASE

I hope you are still keeping an accurate up to date log in your daily planner. The planner is evidence of the actions you take on a daily basis that prove that you have demonstrated reasonable effort.

You can use your daily planner to convey necessary information with your social worker or public defender such as

 dates, times and events etc.

Attendance records for each activity you attend

Certificates are evidence of completion in court, in your case and to some programs for resources and referrals.

Make copies of your lease agreement and proof of employment to show proof of stability.

Letters of Support from counselors and other professionals that are part of your support network.

Bring any other written evidence that shows the courts you are in compliance and you are what is in the best interest of your kids.

Chapter 9

The Pastor and Leading Lady loved seeing my children at church and they showered them with so much love. After church they drove us back to the meet up with the foster mom and watched as we said goodbye.

My children were fairly little, my youngest was still an infant I cradled in my arms. Most of my children were too young to understand what was going on. My six-year-old, Hannah, she knew exactly what was happening and hated saying goodbye. She would hold on to my neck and ask me, why can't we stay at our house now. I reminded her of how far we came. I would say, "remember when you use to only see me for a few hours in the office. Then we went out places and spent more time together.

Now that we have our home and a church family you spend the night and go to church with me. Every time you see me it is just going to get better until finally you do not have to go anymore."

I loved seeing how God was fulfilling His promise to us, but I hated seeing Hannah's heart break every time it was time to go. I kept reminded her you will be home soon. I told her the song we song in church today *How great is our God*. God promised us in that song that all will see, how great is our God. When he brings you all home for good. Every week I reminded her of the song; she dried her eyes, hugged me, smiled and with weighted arms, walked over to the van and cried. I turned and kissed my babies one by one and whispered in their ear I will see you soon. When I looked over at the van, I couldn't see Hannah, I knew she was in the van, but she couldn't bring herself to look back at me again. I took a deep breath allowing my tears to flow as we drove off.

TEMPERANCE

PREDESTINED Woman of Green in Christ Jesus the sky does not set the limits.

PREDESTINED Woman God chose you for His Glory in Christ you are All Sufficient.

You took root in the secret place. You never seek pity or public approval therefore God is breaking ground for you to be seen. You endure the cutting the pruning the bruising the pressing. Through it all you reach for Your Father.

In His presence He meets All your needs.

P.R.E.D.E.S.T.I.N.E.D.

Glory Decree from The Throne of Grace

I AM called you Higher. Higher is your name. Joy is your nature and praise is your posture. I AM is taking you deeper. Surrender everything familiar to you and approach me alone.

I AM taking you where they are not willing to go. I Am nurturing my will inside the depths of your soul. Everything you are experiencing is the nature I declared in you.

I AM called you Higher.

Higher is your name. Every time I call your name you decrease as I increase and show your potential, purpose and strength.

You embody my power use it to stretch higher extend toward heights unimaginable.

I Am your rear guard protecting you from everything that encumbered you.

I Am your source keep your eyes on me.

TRANSFORM

EARNEST PRAYER

I began to pray for my children more earnestly. I know it is God's plan to reunify us, but I also know I was not the best mother and I want to be better. I pray asking God to teach my children to love Him redeem the time loss. I repent again asking God to forgive me for the hurt pain and abuse I caused them.

I remember the parenting class explaining how abusive it is for your children to see you abused because they love you. They talked about how we as parents are not capable of disciplining our children when we are being abused. We become abusive to our children because we are not tuned into their temperament their needs, we just want them to stop.

I thought about how abusive I was to my children instead of disciplining them teaching them or instructing them, I would spank, whoop or send them away. The same way I was brought up before I went into foster care. I remembered my mother and father both were in foster care before and I do not know much about how my grandparents were raised. At that moment as I prayed, I threw it all away.

I told God to teach me how to be a mother even a father. Teach me how to be whatever they need. I asked God to teach me how to discipline. How to teach, instruct and guide my children. I asked God to forgive me for being abusive and intolerant pull all of that out of me and make me new.

I asked God to give my children the heart to forgive me and see me the way he sees me. Not as a victim, abusive, angry or weak. I want my children to see me as a Woman of God. Heal my children from abandonment, pain and abuse. Heal them from instability, insecurity and loss of identity. I said, God cause my children to see themselves the way you see them. My desire is for my children to see themselves as the children of God.

Thank you, Jesus, for hearing my prayer because you have never failed me. In Jesus name, Amen.

IDENTITY

PREDESTINED Woman of Orange nothing seen can define you for it was the will of God that made you.

Predestined Woman

God chose you for His Glory

Your Identity is centered in Christ

You are approved, virtuous, righteous Holy.

I AM not just naming characteristics this is what you are.

You are Wonderfully and Fearfully made.

YES THIS IS WHO YOU ARE

You are Unique

P.R.E.D.E.S.T.I.N.E.D.

Glory Decree from The Throne of Grace

I love you. I see you. I know you from your mother's womb. I fashioned you. I Predestined you, planned everything, laid it out for you. I desire you. I watch over you. I protect you. I am preparing a place for you. When I see the adversary, flesh or the world trying to take away your glory and dominion I fight for you. I hurt when you hurt. I am jealous for you. I cry when you cry, I am so intertwined with you. I am your Father I want only the best for you. I show you the way the truth and the life. I stick by your side when you chose your own path I allow you and with love and mercy I gather you, I wash clean and mend the broken places.

I teach you; I guide you; I nurture you back to health. I remember the good forget the bad.

I AM Your Father Your Loving Dad.

~ GOD

Chapter 10

My children came to stay the night we just finished eating dinner at our dining room table and my eldest daughter Hannah who was six years old at the time. Said mom, God wants some water. I looked at her baffle by the comment and I reached for a water bottle and handed it to her. She said, Mom God cannot drink out of that. I looked at her and paused for a second as she began to laugh because I thought God could drink out of a water bottle. I said, of course not, laughing, what was I thinking?

She said, Mom, when are we coming home?

I said, Ask God.

She said God when are we coming home? She raised her voice excitedly and said, Monday!

She said, we are coming home Monday?

Now asking me.

I said, If God said Monday, then yes, you all are coming home Monday.

With a Sarai kind of sarcasm, (in the Bible where she thought, at my age having a child?) I thought to myself, some Monday. Everyone got down from the table and we finished our nightly routine to get ready for church in the morning.

After Sunday Service, we get in the car with the Pastor and Leading Lady to drop my children off with the foster mom. As we turn into the parking lot of the mall my oldest daughter Hannah sees the van and turns toward me with a gripping hug and said.

"I am not going to cry this time because I am going back to say goodbye to everyone, we are going home tomorrow. They are not going to believe me, but they will see. I am saying bye to everyone at school, my teachers and everyone in my class and at the house so I am not going to cry."

As her mother, I am happy she does not want to cry but I did not know what to say.

I hugged her tight, looking into her eyes I could see her tears full of hope. I wanted to tell her something that would ease the let down because I needed her to be okay if she did not see me tomorrow.

It could be another six days before I see her and I did not want her spirit crushed in hopelessness if it did not turn out the way she said. I mean how could it? I have not gotten a notice from my worker no one is talking about reunification. The first time I am hearing this it is coming out of the mouth of a six-year-old girl, who is saying "Mommy God said we are going home Monday." Now, I see, she believes in God more than me, could, He have told her this?

I cannot take this away from her she is finally strong enough to walk away without crying. I said, "I love you; I love you so much." She got out the car with confidence and walked to the van with a mantra in her heart. She believed this was the last time.

I turned around and kissed each one of my babies, fighting back tears, whispering to them as I always do,

I will see you soon.

One by one hugging them and releasing them back into care.

When I looked out the window of the car Hannah was smiling and waving, she was on a mission to tell everyone bye and expected to come home in less than 24 hours. I wanted to believe with her, but how?

NURTURE

PREDESTINED WOMAN OF BROWN You know when you take care of God's business God takes care of yours in that order. Predestined Woman God chose you for His Glory, Goodness and Mercy shall follow you all the days of your life into eternity.

The Word of God clothed in flesh came down from The Throne, birthed in woman lived a life surrounded by pain, sickness and sin. Dragged away as a criminal, Mocked, beaten and afflicted. Nailed to the cross but not defeated. Ascended Victorious sat on The Throne. His Name is Jesus.

P.R.E.D.E.S.T.I.N.E.D.

Glory Decree from The Throne of Grace

Love others as you Love yourself do not leave The First undone.

Love yourself, for I have loved you.

I chose you not because of my love for me but because of MY Great and Endless love for you.

Keep your eyes on me and you will see yourself the way I see you. I work through you and others see this is true. I have caused them to admire you and the things you do.

You are the daughter of my timing. You know my timing because you are always listening. Ready to hear receive and give.

You will continue to receive because you know the seasons of seed time and harvest.

The earth will yield her strength.

My Word will prove true in every instance.

Take time out for you. Receive from me your portion. You will always have enough to give. Receive my gifts specifically tailored just for you.

Chapter 11

That night I stood in my apartment by myself and I spoke out loud to God. I said, "God you remember that conversation at the dinner table last night? You know the one where you were thirsty. God if you really did tell my daughter she is coming home Monday, as in tomorrow, I need to believe you meant tomorrow. I have court tomorrow. I believe you said Monday…so I guess I am saying I believe you spoke to her and you really wanted some water. I apologize for giving you a closed water bottle. What am I talking about? Okay God. You said Monday, that means tomorrow, help me believe. I began to speak to God in song and in words that cannot be uttered. I began to ask Him to prepare me because I had court in the morning.

I got quiet and I waited because I needed to know if God was giving me my kids back in the morning. I heard in my heart the voice of God and He said, "Let it be according to your faith." I said okay, I can do that! I have faith! Okay God, guide me. He told me do not speak to anyone but me, until I give you the answer, hold on to your faith.

After prayer I wrote down scriptures that would counter the attacks on my faith. I went to court in the morning with a pocket full of scriptures, my folder, and a determination to keep my mouth shut. I spoke only when and how I felt God was releasing me to at that moment. The Public Defender called my name and said follow me. She sat me in a small room, looked at my folder, looked at her folder and said, okay this is how it is going to go in the court. They are returning your kids home to you today. I nearly shouted. I said, Thank You Jesus! She said we are really impressed with all you have accomplished, and we want to see your kids go home.

When I entered court, I walked in calmly and sat down in my chair. The judge started talking to the counselors, social workers, public defenders and other people in the courtroom and then she addressed me and said:

I am impressed with all that you accomplished in this short time.

I am returning your kids to your care.

many women your age and demographic do not do what is necessary; the few that do, end up back here again.

She said firmly:

I do not want to see you back in here again!!!

I said, *Yes*!

Everyone went back to shuffling papers; I looked at my public defender, she said, go back out to the lobby and you will receive your court minutes.

I stepped back into the lobby. My public defender walked out with my court minutes. It was over! I said thank you Jesus as I frantically looked for my phone. I called one of the ladies at the church who strengthened me. I told her my kids are coming home today. She said that is awesome do you have car seats? I said no, I do not. she said, okay I will get them, congratulations. Next, I called the Pastor and told him. He was rejoicing, Glory to God, okay we will be ready to pick up your babies congratulations. I am so proud of you.

It was finally over my daughter was right, they are coming home Monday.

EDIFY

PREDESTINED Woman of light blue You fear God alone and do not desire to please men.

You have One Allegiance to God Your Father and no one else.

God has assigned to you His Decree

Predestined Woman God chose you for His glory because you seek His glory not your own

P.R.E.D.E.S.T.I.N.E.D.

Glory Decree From The Throne Of Grace

Surrounded with people but none can give you guidance. I alone am your resource. My Word will be confirmed. Seek confirmation not instruction I have blocked your sight to open your vision. Things are not as they seem. I called you to Walk by Faith and not by sight. Speak what I showed you and I will bring it to fruition. Step out and I will sustain your feet. Walk in my Word not in the World. You are my Ambassador I alone have called you and qualified you. Do not ask another what they see. I blocked their vision for a season to Glorify MY WORD. You are walking in covenant declaring my promises. Speaking my

Word unveiling my Glory. Creating Testimonies that birth overcomers.

Becoming a Weapon that is forged in fire.

Do not get weary in well doing you will reap the promise for generations after generations. Keep pressing in and yielding to the Holy Spirit there is so much more in store.

Chapter 12

Now Let's Talk About the Enemy

We are given the power to break generational curses by changing generational choices.

Ezekiel 18:20 NKJV

The soul who sins shall die. The son shall not bear the guilt of the father, nor the father bear the guilt of the son. The righteousness of the righteous shall be upon himself, and the wickedness of the wicked shall be upon himself.

²¹ *"But if a wicked man turns from all his sins which he has committed, keeps all My statutes, and does what is lawful and right, he shall surely live; he shall not die.* ²² *None of the transgressions which he has committed shall*

be remembered against him; because of the

righteousness which he has done, he shall live.

23 Do I have any pleasure at all that the wicked

should die?" says the Lord God, "and not that

he should turn from his ways and live?

The doctors say we are susceptible to high cholesterol if our Daddy had it. We are susceptible to heart attacks if our mommy suffered one. Does this mean your immune system is weak or your cardiovascular system has a leak because your mother had a heart attack? Is your brain somehow affected by your Grandmother's nervous breakdown?

Maybe we shake the salt the same way as our Dad instead of grabbing a teaspoon. We react the same way as our mother when we get into a stressful situation. Care too much, work too hard, give people chance after chance that do not deserve the time of day like Grandma did. We stay when we are supposed to go, and we go when we are supposed to stay and all the while we are walking the same figure eight generations before us did. Treading the same path that led them into the messes we only heard bits and pieces of now and then.

I am a daughter of generations of unspeakable sins. Brought out of the comfort of a mother's womb into generations of misplaced trust, molestations, broken marriages, abandonment, children snatched from their parents. Mother's hating their own image in their daughters. Daughters fearful of their mothers.

Children going from day to day never knowing what is going to happen next.

I am a daughter of a Veteran and a praying Mom. I am a granddaughter of a Bishop. Yes the bad always chases the Good. Even the Good Word says, affliction came because of the Word." by and by we are offended. Matthew 13:21 KJV My mother prayed to break generational curses. She woke up early in the morning and went to bed late praying for each of her eight children. My mother wanted her children to be free from the strongholds of the enemy. So, she prayed for us. I believe God answers prayers, so I don't doubt that the chains were broken. The things that took place in my life, the lives of my siblings and my children I must call generational choices. I am not saying we chose our hardships but rather stating that the enemy is cunning and presented the options that created our paths. The enemy laid the snares in our path that we were susceptible to due to the weaknesses of those around us and the emptiness that we felt from our experiences.

I am talking about generational choices that were made as we tried to find love, recover our dignity, gain control and power over what will and will not take place in our lives. The search for our identity as we try to protect the child that was hurt, left alone confused. A child who is waiting for someone to explain what just happened; but it didn't just happen. Tragedy struck years ago but we are still feeling the pain as if it was yesterday. We search for answers in every decision. Some type of answer that will make everything make sense again. Some type of remedy to the pain we feel deep inside. We make choices that we hope will lead to happiness, stability and wholeness. All the while, our bodies betray us running side by side with time, changing but never maturing because without reason, that day, that moment keeps replaying. In reality time is flying and the things generations before us did we are doing never really realizing it is not a generation curse it is a constant presenting of choices that the enemy uses again and again. Like with Adam and Eve. They were told not to eat off the tree. How many times have we been told not to...?

I say it is not a generation curse because I believe God. The Bible says. "Let this proverb no longer be said, "The sins of the Fathers do not fall to the sons." The enemy presented options and solutions and those who bit were led away from God by their desires to be anything but the broken pieces that they felt identified them. However, the enemy's solutions and options gave him access to their lives.

My Father and my Mother got married had children and taught us to love God with all our heart and strength. We all attended church and love filled our home. I truly believe I grew up in a picture perfect home. Nonetheless one thought led to a choice that shattered that home.

Those choices affected everyone and left us all broken inside. Those choices caused us to grow up searching for something anything to cover the hole and stop the bleeding.

I am not my Mother, my Grandmother or anyone from the generations before me but my life began to mirror their hurt, their pain and their childhood experiences. I made decisions that caused my children to know that same pain and loss...two words, BUT GOD! He returned my children home with safe permanency. He stopped the damage and ended the pain. God reversed the outcome and made my family a Sign of Restoration. God taught me how to respond correctly so now I am a beacon of Hope and a Repairer of Breaches. Jesus Christ is the Lord of my battles and battlegrounds.

They call us Victims

but we are

Fighters

and

Victors.

PREDESTINED WOMAN

that is what we are.

DESTINY

Predestined Woman of Gold you are the manifestation of Beauty for Ashes.

Predestined Woman God chose you for His Glory you have gone too far to turn back now.

With your destiny comes divine direction and provision. God is leading you in unexplainable ways through uncharted territory. Continue to trust God as He reveals to you His glory.

From the desert to the promise your road is not easy but when you see where God is taking you, you will be able to look back at the journey from start to finish.

P.R.E.D.E.S.T.I.N.E.D.

Glory Decree From The Throne Of Grace

You said, *Yes, So I Am Giving It All To You*

You Yield Yourself to *All That I Am*.

Consistently, seeking my face.

I AM revealing the place that I AM preparing for you.

YOU ARE Exemplifying courage.

I AM GIVING you The Faith exchange.

You are placing your hope in me and allowing your vision to become my vision so I AM opening up heaven to you.

I AM opening your Eyes to see revelation in the face of reality.

I AM opening your Ears to Hear the wind words. I AM keeping your heart compassionate and understanding. I AM releasing it all to you and so much more.

You said Yes so I AM giving it all to you.

Are You A Witness

From Ashes to Beauty God has rewrote your story. From mourning to rejoicing everything is shifting. One decision gave you the strength to hold on until your hope manifested into blessings. You can now see your way out of the schemes and plots of the enemy. Your voice has returned, and you are not afraid to reach out for help. Did you see it happening? Did you feel your growth as you reached for heights once unimaginable?

You are a witness, if God can do it for you, He can do it for anyone who is not ashamed to put their trust in Him. Now you know fear did not put you on this journey; faith did. Courage caused you to stand before the courts and show up for your kids. Full of strength you laughed in the face of fear and said, "I AM Victorious."

You pressed through declaring the outcome standing on faith believing the seeds you sowed of good will one day reap a harvest. When others would give up, you held on and received more than you could ever expect or feel you deserve. You know who you are, and who's you are, but how many more need to know? How many more could benefit from your story? I invite you once again to find the greatest version of yourself. Are you ready? To restore, rebuild and renew you? Are you ready to continue the journey of pursuing every opportunity presented to you, to reclaim your life and do what you are PREDESTINED TO

DO!

PREDESTINED GLORY DECREE

FROM THE THRONE OF GRACE

Complete but yet unveiling.

Perfectly designed.

A masterpiece of my own creation.

I AM yours and you are mine.

Day by day your beauty unlocks.

Emerging from the depths of intimacy.

We both wait with patience to see the fullness

of Unconditional Love.

My Image is reflected in the way you speak.

You are determined and breaking chains,

thriving in my Sovereignty.

I AM preparing you to endure to the end, to live in abundance in Jesus name.

I AM sharpening your awareness of the things that endeavor to make you complacent.

I AM unleashing The Now Word repeatedly refreshing your desperation,

Receive My Spoken Word above the Gift of Wisdom.

You are a champion in righteousness proclaim

I AM PREDESTINED WOMAN

This is what we do, we restore confidence, trust and identity back into the lives of mothers while building support networks, expecting reunification and encouraging women to become a leader in their church and communities.

There is something we can do now in our churches to help women and children reunite with their family with safe permanency. Women's groups can become a way for women to connect with Godly accountability partners who won't judge them for what they are going through, instead they see the generational impact their triumph will have on their lives. The women's group can become a connection to people they can share their accomplishments with step by step and be cheered on to grow their self-esteem.

Many women who grew up in instability and Children Family Services have never celebrated their successes in life. Many never heard words addressed to them like the ones in this book.

No one said good job, you can do it, I believe in you because nothing was ever good enough. Hearing you are beautiful struck fear in their heart because it was coming from someone with ill intentions. I lived this way for a long time but God has a way of breathing new life into us through His word. His word causes us to try again with a new-found Hope.

Connect with I AM PREDESTINED we are expanding to reach women all over the world to build a solid support team for women who experienced separation and are seeking reunification and restoration.

Give the women in your group a worldwide support network that will cheer for them every step of the way. Women going through reunification need more than family and friends they are in the fight for their life and the lives of their children. The mothers need to be immersed with love and support and able to socialize with people who will speak life to them that understand the process of reunification and restoration.

Contact I AM PREDESTINED on Facebook and find out how you can create a woman's group to help women reunify with their children.

It is nearly impossible to write all the things my children and I experienced before I gave my life to Christ and all the people and words of encouragement we received on our journey to Beauty for Ashes. I thank God for everyone that helped us along the way. I blame no one. Everyone who ever hurt me helped me intentionally in more ways than they hurt me and everything that they did that caused me pain or shame God turned around for my establishment.

I would like for women to be restored with their children once again. I want to see families made new in Christ. If you want that too here is one thing you can do now.

Connect the women you know going through the reunification process with I AM PREDESTINED we are creating ways to empower and restore women and their families throughout the reconciliation and restoration process to wholeness.

In 2017-2018 we helped women reunify with their kids through community, prayer and resources. Now we are launching our social media platforms. Maybe you are a woman who experienced domestic violence, recently reunified with your children or grew up in foster homes/group homes and you can relate with a lot of the things I mentioned in this book. You do not feel whole, you are seeking identity, stability and purpose.

I am personally connecting with women just like you all over the world. I give credit to God for breaking the cycle of instability, abuse and fear in my life and the lives of my children. Now I am stepping out to help break the cycle in others. Women who need to be around people who see the best in them. The groups that I am putting together to support you will never judge you because we were you. We see where God is taking you. Connect with us through Facebook This is only the beginning.

Maybe you are saying I never experienced any of this but I work in this industry. I see people like this daily.

You may be a foster mom, or you license foster moms. Where ever you work or volunteer you want to be a part of the solution reunifying mothers with their children. You can connect with I AM PREDESTINED we are currently working with several foster moms and they are doing amazing things and seeing reunification with no shortage of children still coming through their doors, but now leaving with smiles, identity, hope and wholeness.

You may not fit in any of these categories mentioned but you still want to be a part of this growing ministry making a global impact in the world. Please reach out to I AM PREDESTINED and become a Generational influence in families lives. We welcome you!

The church is an integral part of my journey and is still my lifeline now. Women who are going through domestic violence and trying desperately to reunify with their children need to know the church is their lifeline. Churches need to hear more stories like mine to understand the impact that they make on an ordinary Sunday service is nothing short of Extraordinary.

The program that provided my apartment lost their funding to help women in my situation. The funding went to a serious epidemic of chronic homelessness in our county. I believe the reason the funding went to another cause is because they did not understand the impact helping a woman reunify with her children can has on our global economy.

The church on the other hand, understood when they encouraged me they were making an eternal impact in me and my children. The type of impact that changes a woman, a family, generations, even communities.

Women who receive love and support from their church do not just say thank you and leave. I went out and told others by joining prayer walks in my community. I brought people who lived in my local community into the church to be healed and set free. I told my mother, my father, my brothers, and sisters, they all attended the church. The pastor performed my eldest brother's wedding and he became the sound engineer and now the Sunday School and Bible Study Teacher. His wife and daughter are proud to call the church their home and tell others about the good news of Jesus Christ.

There are community and government resources available for women working toward family reunification, but I know by experience that resources are not enough. Women need a strong support team and I found mine in Christ. I mentioned earlier, I met other young ladies like me along the way. Later I learned they did not reunify with their children. The judge I mentioned in my case said few women have the success I had and those that do bring their children home most often end up back in court. I believe what separates the few that have reunified with their children and restored their family bond is The Church.

It all starts with God and the Body of Christ. He

is the source and resource.

Made in the USA
Middletown, DE
02 October 2021